A to Z of

All of Me

Tracy Nelson Maurer

Rourke Publishing LLC
Vero Beach, Florida 32964

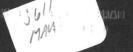

About The Author:

Tracy Nelson Maurer specializes in nonfiction and business writing. Her most recently published children's books include the Green Thumb Guides series, also from the Rourke Book Company. A University of Minnesota graduate, Tracy lives with her husband Mike and two children in Superior, Wisconsin.

Acknowledgments:

With appreciation to Margaret and Thomas for their joyful assistance in developing this series, and to Lois M. Nelson for her editing and enthusiastic support.

PHOTO CREDITS:
© Photodisc, cover; © Linda Dingman, page 13, 16, 22, 26; © Diane Farleo, 6, 40, 48; © Julie Johanik, page 20, 25;
© Lois M. Nelson, page 4, 8, 10, 12, 14, 18, 24, 28, 30, 32, 34, 26, (37?*), 38, 42, 44, 46.

Library of Congress Cataloging-in-Publication Data

Maurer, Tracy, 1965–
    A to Z of all of me / Tracy Nelson Maurer.
        p. cm. — (A to Z)
    ISBN 1-58952-059-9
    1. Body, human—Juvenile literature. 2. Human anatomy—Juvenile literature. [1. Body, human. 2. Alphabet] I. Title

QM27 .M38 2001
611—dc21

2001018588

Printed in the USA

Know Your Body from Head to Toe

Your body uses all kinds of parts to keep you moving and to keep you healthy. Follow the alphabet to name many of them. You'll think of others, too. Remember, take good care of your body from head to toe with a healthy diet and fun exercise!

Aa

Arms give great big hugs.

Bb

Brains win games.

Cc

Calves are leg muscles.

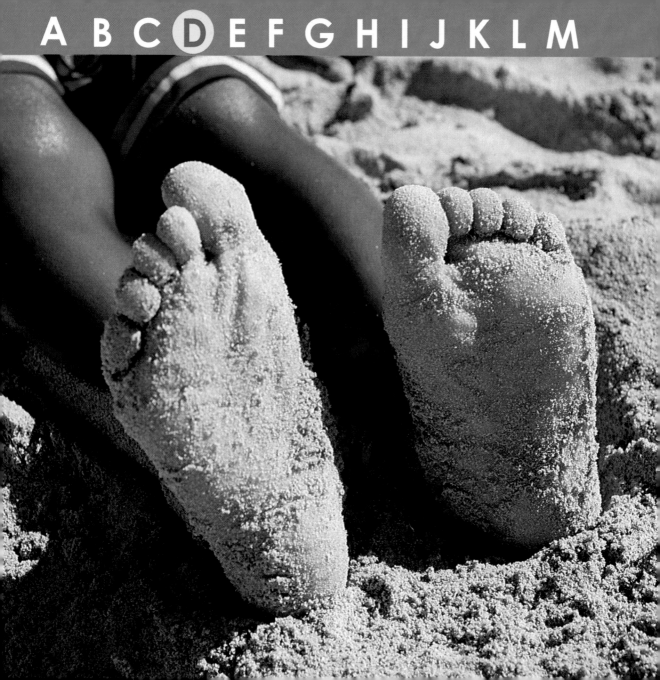

Dd

Digits are your fingers and toes.

Ee

Elbows let your arms bend.

12

Ff

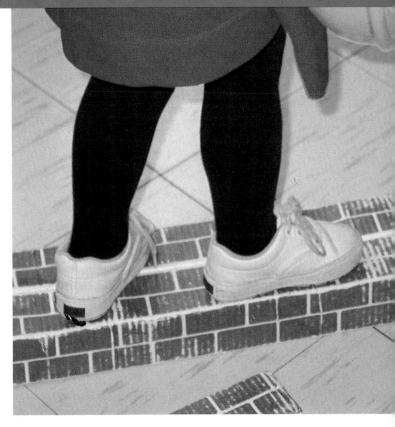

Feet help you balance.

13

Gg

Gaps show if teeth fall out.

ABCDEFG**H**IJKLM

Hh

Hands paint pictures.

Ii

Iris is the eye's colored part.

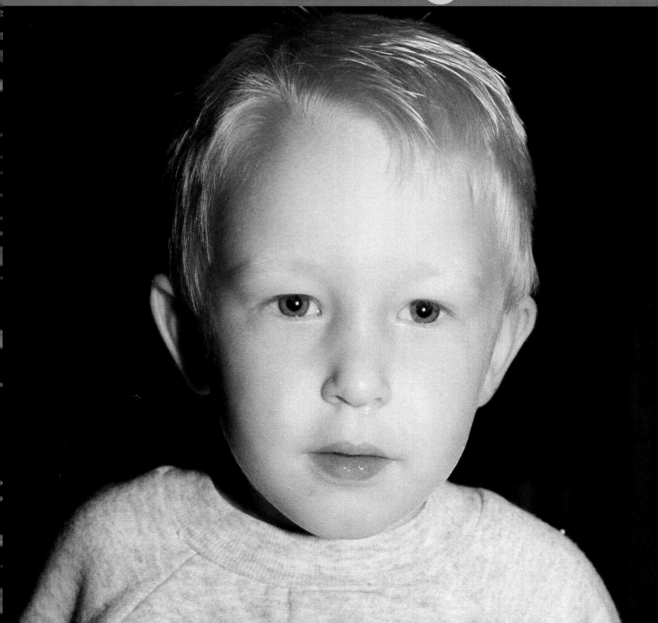

ABCDEFGHI**J**KLM

Jj

Jawbones shape your face.

Kk

Knees bend when you crawl.

Ll

Lips put a smile on your face.

24

Mm

Muscles help you lift things.

Nn

Noses run in the cold air.

Oxygen keeps you alive.

A B C D E F G H I J K L M

Pp

Pupils let in light to see.

ABCDEFGHIJKLM

Quadriceps are thigh muscles.

33

ABCDEFGHIJKLM

Rr

Ribs protect your heart.

Ss

Skin holds your insides in.

Tt

Thumbs up for a job well done.

ABCDEFGHIJKLM

Uu

Underarms are ticklish.

Vv

Veins carry blood.

Ww

Wrist action moves the paddle.

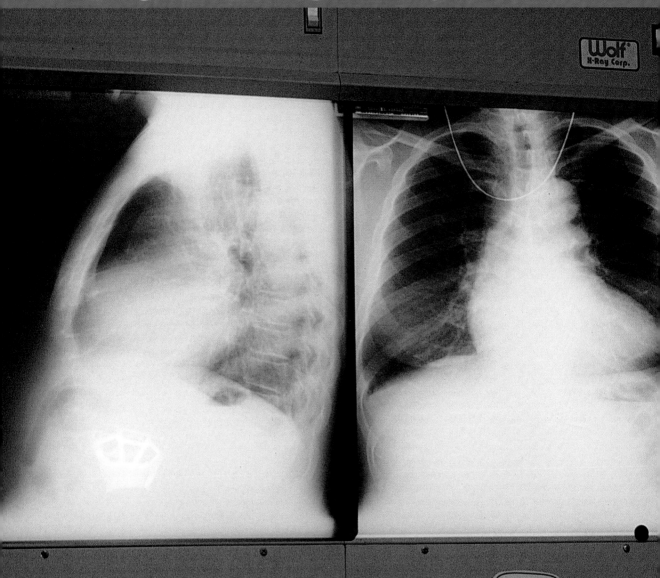

X-rays show inside your body.

A B C D E F G H I J K L M

Yy

You! No one else is like you.

Zz

Z, Z, Z, Zs — Sleep well!